Text by Gilles Clément
Graphics by Vincent Gravé

A Big Garden

Prestel

Munich · London · New York

May Garden

The very first garden in history was filled with vegetables and fruits:
a crop garden.

It started out when people began to settle the land. Previously, they were nomadic.

Nomads roam about looking for fruits and vegetables in the wild. They do not have gardens.
The settlers began going in search of seeds and plants that would bear them things to eat.
They then sowed and planted them in a closed, protected area: the garden.
In earlier times, they would find seeds and shoots in the natural habitat, near to their village or even farther away, when they were traveling.
They were gathering.
Nowadays, of course, people visit stores for their food.
They go shopping.

To create a garden, the gardener needs to arrange the area: he makes lines, squares and sections.
Then he has to figure out how to arrange his crops.
At first, he might separate the different vegetables and trees he has decided to grow.
He could also change his mind and mix all the plants together. The vegetables would grow just as well, maybe even better. But they would be more complicated to maintain, water and harvest.
At last, the gardener comes upon the best option. He groups his plants according to type and creates a system.

He chooses his seeds, paying careful attention to the climates and seasons in which they will grow best. A seedbed cannot simply be planted at any time of year, so the gardener keeps a diary to write down his planting schedule.

He always has his hands in the soil and looks up to the sky.

Can you spot a fox, a squirrel,
a cat and a mouse?
What other animals can you find?

June Fruit

The gardener sows and harvests.

But he does more than just that.

From the moment he plants to the day he harvests, days and months pass by. This is a time of growth, transformation and development. Everything goes well, as long as the weeds don't overrun the plants, the birds don't steal the seeds, the rabbits don't make nests in the onion patch, the mole doesn't build a tunnel beneath the radishes, the crickets dutifully eat the aphids and the rain falls gently and regularly.

In the time from first planting his seeds to harvesting his crop, the gardener observes, stands in awe and … simply gets on with his gardening.

Put simply, gardening is all about interpreting the future and overcoming the unforeseeable.

The gardener is required to:
– remove any grass that might hamper the seedlings;
– fetch water when things get too dry;
– prop up any plant that cannot stand by itself;
– return the mulch the fox has disturbed below the tomatoes;
– protect a hitherto unknown species, new and in full bloom. How did that get there?;
– harvest the lettuce before it goes to seed;
– cut back the apple tree and remove the deadwood;
– hang up a worn CD that shimmers in the sunlight and distracts the birds from stealing cherries;
– pick fruit at just the right time …

The long awaited fruits are watched while they grow until their color indicates they are ripe and ready to eat.

Some untended fruits appear in the middle of summer on the ends of thorny bramble branches. Blackberries, wild strawberries, blueberries, walnuts, chestnuts, medlar cherry fruits, hazelnuts, Cornelian cherries … these fruits are picked as a gift.

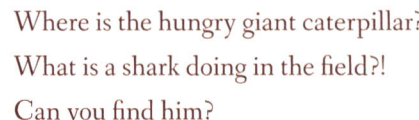

Where is the hungry giant caterpillar?
What is a shark doing in the field?!
Can you find him?

July Sun

The gardener works the soil.

He understands the importance of the soil – its richness, its being. However, he does not see all the remarkable things that happen underground to make plant growing possible.
One day, he would like to visit this concealed world.

There, he could discover in full astonishment how the roots intertwine like a labyrinth or an obstacle course. He would understand how the roots of different plants have their own space, growing and co-existing here without contact ...

He would also learn how some plants achieve mastery over others.
How is it that one species can frighten another and cause it to move away, without even budging from its own place in the ground?
It is said that the hawkweed emits poison from the end of its roots to fend off grass ...
It is also said that leeks like strawberries ...

Our gardener would see a diversity of plant forms. He is familiar with some of the things he harvests: the smooth round onion, for example.
He knows the roughness of the beetroot, the well-anchored stem of the carrot and the full surface of the leek.
He also understands the variable shapes of potatoes: their false roots and swollen stems, their edible tubers hidden in the soil.

If the land is alive and well, and if the gardener has not dumped chemicals that may harm it, then he can see a wealth of animal life in his garden: friendly earthworms and moth chrysalises, as well as the less-cherished grubs and snail eggs.

Using a microscope, he can also see a billion bacteria.

In other words, all that gives life is visible in a garden.

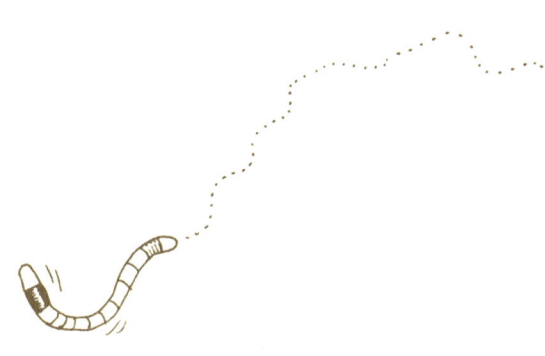

Can you spot carrots, leeks, potatoes and beetroots in the garden?
Do you see a gemstone?

August Forest of Flowers

The forest of flowers is a blossoming meadowland as seen from a rabbit's perspective ... or even that of an ant.

Everything seems strange when seen "up close" with a detailed, fixed gaze.

The gardener often gets close to the ground, and he sometimes sticks his nose into the flowers. But his eyes are not designed to perceive the world as rabbits and ants do. He therefore has to imagine he is a rabbit, an ant or even a ladybug to recognize the exact map of plant species in this meadow.

The ants know that a very clear space separates each species: terrain that is lined by littered straw, which is ideal for tracing the ants' paths.

The rabbit is interested in the different textures: it pushes the spiky thorns, the dry grass and rough bark aside to taste the succulent, tender grass.

A variety of fragrances exist that the gardener does not recognize, yet a host of animals come to seek them out.

Each species emits a range of scents that alert the noses of others.

Attracted by the odors of the sepals and the sweetness of the nectar, insects love to drop in on flowers. The flowers, in turn, need the insects to transport their pollen to other flowers.

Some fragrances deter raiders – plants have to protect themselves the best way they can. They cannot run away.

Plants interact with other creatures in remarkable ways.
They create music, they give off electrical currents and they communicate.

The forest of flowers amazes the gardener who opens his eyes as if he were a rabbit or ant. He does not comprehend everything, but everything interests him.

Then he lies down among flowers and listens. He also tries to communicate with them to the best of his abilities.

Sometimes he falls asleep.

Do you see the trumpet flower?
Where is the umbrella?

September Character of the Gardener

The gardener can do anything others can do, such as:
– wear a straw hat
– stretch his arms to the sky
– ignite a bomb
– charm a snake
– dry his laundry
– play the trumpet
– catch a butterfly
– paint a Picasso
– ward off the moon
– frame a picture
– go on fire
– start sprouting leaves
– present himself as a gift
– pretend to be a cat, rat, rabbit, wolf, devil, hedgehog, mouse or angel
– get mummified
– wear a top hat
– be on time
– fall in love
– dance
– go hiking
– push a wheelbarrow
– make a call saying: ring, ring!
– hand over a tulip
– lose his head ...

Yet, he is the only one gardening.

You see that, right?

Can you discover a snake, a pumpkin head and a spider's web?

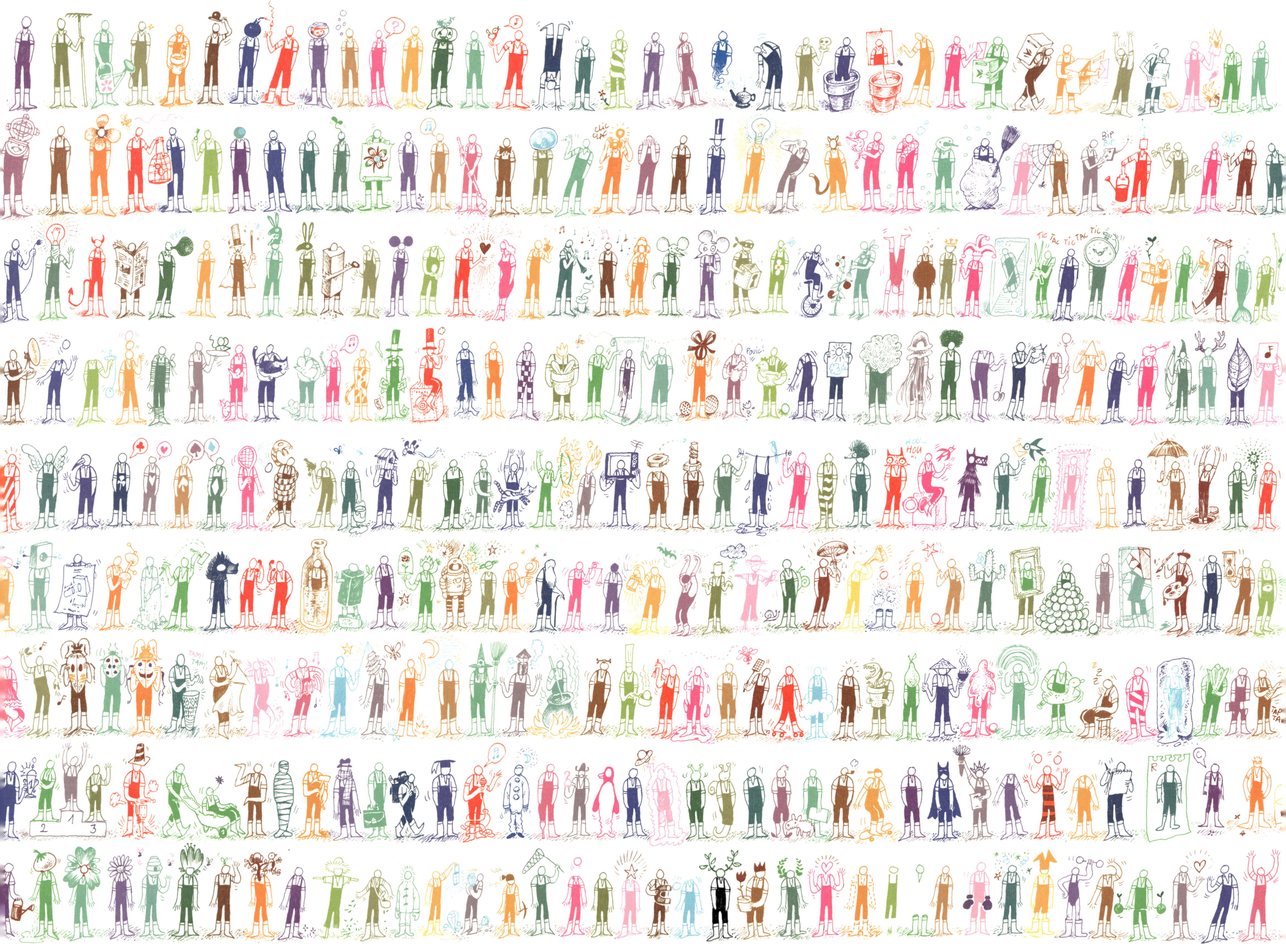

October Mushrooms

Mushrooms are not animals and they are not plants.
Mushrooms are mushrooms.

They reign apart.

They are part of a group of remarkable living things called saprophytes, better known as fungi. Fungi exist in the company of other beings, accompanying them or living off of them.

They sometimes live alone, especially the very big ones.

We should recognize them more than we do. They show off their beautiful hats, their stalk-like parasols (umbels), their delicate tissued caps and their coral-like shapes. But their appearances are quite temporary.
They spring up when it is time to fertilize, only for a few days or weeks towards the end of summer when the autumn rains are beginning to refresh the soil.
For the rest of the year, mushrooms remain silent, invisible and underground.

They live in fibrous blankets in the deep, thick soil. Only animals below the surface of the earth know them well. Worms, larvae, ants, springtails ... they all encounter mushrooms in their underground form (mycelium), and they sometimes feed on them.

Some mushrooms never even appear at ground level. They are content with a life away from light, mating and reproducing oblivious to the sun. Some live in contact with the roots of trees and grass, which is good in times of drought because their roots know how to hold water. Plants need these invisible mushrooms.

Their beautiful hats, known as carpophores, resemble trumpets or umbrellas.
They can be brown, pink, beige or red. Sometimes they are spotted and sometimes striped, but they are always fleshy – a perfect texture for the savory mushroom dishes we like to cook.

Slugs, snails, ants and termites are also keen on mushrooms ... and they do not need to do any cooking to enjoy them as a good meal.

In our woodlands, wild boars, foxes and squirrels all share the same taste we do for parasol mushrooms, ceps and chanterelles.

It is said that deer also love chanterelles.

Well, the gardener does, too.

An accident occurred while painting the fly agaric mushroom! Can you find out what happened?

November Winter

In winter, the gardener takes a vacation.

The leaves have fallen, fruits have been harvested, as have the green roots of the vegetable patch.

A few cabbages, winter and lamb's lettuce, beet, salsify and carrots remain in the soil.
Some late and rare crops will be harvested only if the weather permits.

The trees and herbs are asleep. The woods are clear and brightness crosses through the forests.
The scene has changed and you can see much farther. Nothing could hinder the view if it were not for the wood of the pines, the hardy hollies and the stone walls. Winter changes little in this town.

Snow falls.

Everything seems to stop and everything begins.

This is a blank sheet on which everything can be written – because everything can be seen as never before.

Traces of foxes, weasels and martens appear now and then. We know they live among us throughout the year, but now we can see them and trace their paths.

The robin swells with down to protect it from the cold.
The disheveled squirrel leaves its hideout in quest of an acorn.
The raven appears to be twice its size.
Insects, lizards and snakes have all disappeared.
The whimpering cry of a black woodpecker and the call of the tawny-owl can be heard at nightfall.
Winter is believed to be silent, yet it is punctuated by separate, clear and repeated songs.

These are the conversations heard in cold countries during the winter. Only when spring returns will the animals from the South, the seasonal migrants, make their appearance here.

Do you see the snowman and the skier?

December Gaze of Winter

The gardener may be on holiday, but he is now able to dream, sleep, walk about and see everything around him that suddenly appears from under the snow – things he had never seen before.

Up in the gardener's library, there is a book that he should not be without: it is the book on tracking.
It's a veritable winter game: how to recognize the animals around here, hidden during daytime, yet still very much present. The clue lies in the traces they leave on the ground. Paw marks, signs of litter and bedding, solitary droppings – every single object is a form of identification.

There are other games, too. Snow is another water sport.
Legend says that this slightly cold, compressible and malleable material was invented just to amuse children.
Snow brings out the youngster who remains within us.
It makes us scream, slide and make snowballs.
Sometimes, we dress it up as snowmen and other fantastic creatures.

And after making snowballs, you can play the only war game worth winning: the snowball fights where the sole form of suffering is death by laughter!
In these clashes, the explosion of the snow 'bomb' is accompanied by giggles and screams of joy.

Winter is a big animal who pretends to sleep under thick sheets of snow or dead leaves. It watches secretly how we are amused by it or suffer from it with just one eye open.
It remains discreet, invisible to some of us. It sees how some of us become bored and demanding, while others feel the days are too short and the nights are pretty. And for the gardener, winter arranges a careful transformation.
It enables him to prepare for spring (something called vernalization in books), a period when he exposes his seeds to the cold so that they will awaken and sprout more swiftly in the spring.

The gardener waits. He knows he will be surprised. Every year, the list of plants springing up by the time the snow has melted increases.

Life is a permanent invention.

Can you find a winter animal in hiding?
Where is Little Red Riding Hood?

January Thaw

The thawing of the ice signals the end of winter.
The gardener of the crop garden is delighted because he can now think about planting tomatoes.

It is a different story for the planetary gardener, the inhabitant of the Earth.
That's because the snow and ice melts have accelerated to the point where the sea is rising into our living rooms.

Water trapped by glaciers, pack ice and perpetual snowfall have accumulated at the lowest part of Earth – namely, the great oceans between our continents.
It is eating away at the coastlines, flooding villages and drowning the ground floor of the town hall.
Scandalous!

How should we face climate change?
Well, those Earth dwellers who've built their houses by the seas and rivers will have to learn to swim, build boats or move elsewhere.

Their gardens are vanishing under water.

Is it possible to create a marine garden?

Without doubt, but who would be the gardeners to tend it?
Which colleges will teach us how to build aquatic pergolas so we can observe and reproduce its plants and animals?
How can we explore the richness of marine life in order to better understand and protect it? And how can we protect it by not getting into the water?

We are experimenting at breeding fish, oysters and seaweed. Maybe that's just a start.
Should we begin exploring the great shoals and abysses of the deep?

Can we avoid damaging our oceans by preventing oil spillage, floating waste piles and chemical pollution?

For the sea is liquid soil full of hidden species.
And the power of moving water in the ocean can overwhelm anything on land:
a small bit of earth or a mountain,
a dead leaf or a forest,
a poison or a fertilizer.

The flood gardener will need to know how to row.

And with time, he will have gills.

Can you spot a sunken ship?

February Insects

The gardener, of course, will look after his gardens.
But he is also a caretaker for all living things.
He does all he can to avoid harming those animals that occupy his space.
The gardener does not use any chemicals whatsoever that might suppress growth in his garden.

That's why insects exist – they rustle about night and day.
In the clearings, at the edges of woods, in the crop garden, among the flowers, in the grass and in the trees
– they fly about everywhere.

We hear the shrill of crickets and locusts, especially during high summer, as well as the squealing
buzz of the cicadas and the engine sound of Lucas insects and rose chafers at dusk.

Flies, gadflies, bugs, wasps and bees are buzzing. And don't forget those irritating mosquitoes!
Only butterflies and ichneumon wasps remain unobtrusive. They are not heard; they are seen.

We are astonished by their beauty, yet we do not grasp why they display such a vast array of colors and shapes.
We venture to guess why these flying insects only survive for such a short period of time. They take on this elegant
form for only part of their lives.
The dancing flight of the newly hatched Vanessa butterfly, with its red and black ocher shades, is part of the
final journey of its life. She has wings to find a mate in this field of flowers.
Before hatching, however, she was an earthbound caterpillar grazing on the nearest leaves at hand.
What a transformation!

The gardener would love to possess the magic powers of insects: the agility of an Old World swallowtail butterfly, the
swiftness of a sphynx moth and the serenity of a blowfly hovering from one side of the field to the other without
flapping its wings.
He would like to have a shielded breastplate like the beetles, with their skeleton on the outside. Then, there would
be no need for boots, aprons, hats and gloves to protect his fragile skin from the sun's rays.
Above all, though, the gardener would love to fly slowly and look at the countryside from above, using only air as his
support. For air, in fact, is not just empty space; it can support a flying creature.

Nothing is immaterial in the eyes of the gardener.
And nothing is more solid when it comes to the flying insect.

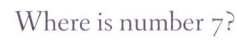

Where is number 7?

March Easter Eggs

Springtime is here. The birds return with their songs, cries, hollers, flights and gatherings, all in the effort to find a mate and create little ones.

The migrants have arrived. They settle down. The natives wake up. Everyone sniffles, whisks about and reproduces. There are eggs everywhere.

Not all of them are worthwhile. Not every one of them will become a newly hatched baby. There are sterile eggs within frogs, broken eggs with some birds and eggs overrun by insects. There are even egg thieves, and we are among them.

When the eggshells shatter, the offspring appear.
Surprised by the light and their surroundings, these new animals come to life. Everything begins to take shape in spring.

There are multicolored eggs, packaged eggs, eggs in silver foil and even those made of chocolate and biscuits. There are fabricated eggs. There are gift-wrapped eggs and boxed ones, too, as well as Russian doll eggs housing still smaller ones.

Some eggs are on full show and others are hidden: for it's now Easter and we have to find them!

The quest is on, exploring and traipsing over trails, searching the lawns and peeking behind the shrubbery: this is all part of the discovery of the garden.

Like Tom Thumb, the gardener sows the eggs. He defines the route and organizes the visit to his kingdom, yet he does not make an appearance himself.

There is no map for this trip through the labyrinth.

It is a treasure hunt.

Not all treasures are made of chocolate, though.

The sight of buttercups in bloom can be a wonderful Easter present in itself!

Can you find the egg painter?
How about the photographer?

April Bloom

Flowers come in all shapes and colors.

So remarkable and easy to arrange, they provide inspiration to many a botanist (or plant scientist). Botanists have categorized plants – each and every one of them – into families according to the shapes of their flowers.

The legume species papilionaceae (nowadays fabaceae), which includes sweet-peas and beans, has flowers that look like butterflies' wings.
Umbellifers (nowadays apiaceous) include carrots and fennel, and their flowers resemble an umbrella.
A crucifer (nowadays brassicaceae), such as Dame's rocket or mustard, produces a four-petalled flower in the shape of a cross.

A composite (nowadays asteraceae) is a plant with multiple flowers that are assembled to look like a single blossom.

Daisies are the best-known asters, because we like to pluck them when singing: 'She loves me, she loves me not ...'

The composite blossom of a daisy contains two distinct flower types: the small flowers that make up the round center and the long, petal-shaped flowers that decorate the edge. Composites radiate so vividly, they remind us of the sun or the stars. That's why we call them asters.

The gardener keeps an eye on the stars. His gardening schedule is linked to the course of the stars, the moon and the sun.

The gardener loves composite flowers because they depend on the stars, sun and moon.

Which gardener watches the stars?

© for the French edition: Cambourakis, 2016
Title of the original edition: Un grand jardin
© for the English edition: 2018, Prestel Verlag, Munich · London · New York
A member of Verlagsgruppe Random House GmbH
Neumarkter Strasse 28 · 81673 Munich
This edition was published in agreement with The Picture Book Agency, France. All rights reserved.

Prestel Publishing Ltd.
14-17 Wells Street
London W1T 3PD

Prestel Publishing
900 Broadway, Suite 603
New York, NY 10003

In respect to links in the book, the Publisher expressly notes that no illegal content was discernible on the linked sites at the time the links were created.
The Publisher has no influence at all over the current and future design, content or authorship of the linked sites. For this reason the Publisher expressly disassociates itself from all content on linked sites that has been altered since the link was created and assumes no liability for such content.

Library of Congress Control Number: 2017950207
A CIP catalogue record for this book is available from the British Library.

Translated from the French by Paul Kelly
Copyediting: Brad Finger
Production management: Corinna Pickart
Printing and binding: Tien Wah Press
Paper: Tauro

Verlagsgruppe Random House FSC® N001967

Printed in Malaysia

ISBN 978-3-7913-7332-4
www.prestel.com